IMOINDA: Or She Who Will Lose Her Name
A play for twelve voices in three acts

IMOINDA: Or She Who Will Lose Her Name
A play for twelve voices in three acts

By Joan Anim-Addo

MANGO PUBLISHING
2008

Published by Mango Publishing, London UK
P.O. Box 13378, London SE27 OZN
email: info@mangoprint.com
website: www.mangoprint.com

ISBN 1 902294 39 4
EAN 9781902294 39 1
British Library Cataloguing in Publication Data
A CIP catalogue record for this book is available from the British Library

Printed by J.H. Haynes & Co. Ltd., Sparkford
Cover design by Raimi Gbadamosi
Acknowledgements: Oleg Maslyakov and Tsvik Yefim, 'Good Morning Africa'

CHARACTER LIST

IMOINDA, a maiden of the court

ESTEIZME, her maidservant

PRINCE OKO, heir to the throne

BAKU, tutor to Prince Oko

CHIEF MOURNER, an old woman

MESSENGER, an old man attached to the court

KING, sovereign of mythical Guinea

CHIEF, a rival and neighbour

DRIVER, slave driver elevated from among the slaves

OVERSEER, white man in charge of the day to day working of the plantation

SAILOR/PLANTER, a white man

WOMEN, spirit of the land

CHORUS involves all members of the cast variously in each act.

AUTHOR'S NOTE
This play was first published in a bi-lingual edition (English and Italian), *Imoinda — Or She Who Will Lose Her Name: A Play for Twelve Voices in Three Acts*. In Covi, Giovanna, ed., *Voci femminili caraibiche e interculturalita*, Trento, Italy: *I Labirinti*, Publicazzioni Università di Trento, 2003: Appendix, 1-155.

ACT ONE
Loves Young and Old — The Old Country

Scene 1: "I am no stranger to death"
Old Guinea. The home of Papa General, great warrior of the Kromanti people of mythical Guinea. The sound of women's wailing and drums are heard in the distance. CHORUS winds its way backstage. MUSIC — "Triumph of Manhood".

CHORUS: *(MUSIC — "Triumph of Manhood")*
>Such a son! Such a son!
>When a nation loses such a son!
>Such a son! A triumph of manhood!
>One who fights like the fiercest lion.
>A son of honour! Triumph of manhood!
>Natural warrior amongst warriors.
>A son of honour! Triumph of manhood!
>Must not all the nation weep as one?

Enters IMOINDA front stage. She startles her MAID who gazes into a calabash of water. MUSIC — Loud gong followed by drums.

IMOINDA:
>Come, Esteizme. I can wait no more.
>Come. About the corn row, I'd say start
>with a parting in the middle. Then
>make all the plaits travel uphill. Come.

MAID: *(Faintly)*
>Coming.

IMOINDA:
>Fear sits in your eyes like a frightened bird
>again. This will not do. Listen!
>What you hear is only the chorus

that announces death. It is not
death itself.

CHORUS: *(MUSIC - "When Time's Ripe")*
　　When the time's ripe, we will know.
　　Why listen for death?
　　When the time's ripe, we will know.
　　Why listen for death?

IMOINDA:
　　Tell me why Esteizme?
　　Why listen for death?
　　Who walks that way, walks alone.
　　Why listen for death?

MAID:
　　My burden is seeing far;
　　Watching over you.
　　My burden is seeing far;
　　Watching over you.
　　So that you can grow, I wait;
　　Watching over you.

IMOINDA:
　　When the time comes, who can tell?
　　Why listen for death?

MAID:
　　But, madam . . .

IMOINDA:
　　Hush. Has this village not bred warriors
　　renowned throughout this forest land?
　　Death itself is not the final victor,
　　remember. Rather, think upon
　　he who speeds the arrow.

MAID:
> Sure, your father . . .

IMOINDA:
> My father? Of course, but why do you speak
> of my father whilst fear widens your eyes?
> Look how fear sparks there. Esteizme, speak!

MAID:
> Not three suns away,
> a shadow passed over this compound.

IMOINDA:
> Yes. What kind of shadow? *(Drums and wailing nearer)*

MAID:
> A chill shadow, madam.
> Your father came into my heart.
> It seemed he left a message on the wind,
> a message for you.

IMOINDA:
> A message? And why did you not tell me?

MAID:
> Tell you, young lioness?
> And unstopper the gourd of sorrow?
> I could not.

IMOINDA:
> Look at me. I am no longer a child.
> What can sorrow do to me?
> I know its taste can only last so long.

(CHORUS and official mourning party approach. MUSIC — drums & wailing)

CHIEF MOURNER: *(Enters)*
    Where is she who answers to the name
    Imoinda?
    She whose father, mighty general,
    Papa General,
    kept our enemies licking their own wounds?
    Where is she who answers to the name
    Imoinda?

IMOINDA: *(To MAID)*
    Why did you not tell me?
    I could have prepared myself. *(Drums)*

CHIEF MOURNER:
    Daughter of the lion of Kromanti,
    accept your father's funeral cloth.
    He left to fight our proud nation's wars
    and stayed to speak with the ancestors
    of his many noble deeds. *(DANCE - "War Victory")*

CHORUS:
    (SONG — "Triumph of Manhood")
    When a nation loses such a son,
    a triumph of manhood,
    one who fights like the fiercest lion,
    natural warrior amongst warriors,
    a triumph of manhood,
    must not all the nation weep as one?

    Daughter of the lion of Kromanti,
    a triumph of manhood,
    take pride in a father amongst fathers,
    great defender of the nation,
    a triumph of manhood,
    leader of young men into battle.

Act One Scene 1

CHIEF MOURNER:
>Imoinda, wind your father's
>funeral cloth about your person.
>Our great Lion marches on his way.
>Elders nod at mention of his name.

CHORUS:
>A triumph of manhood!

CHIEF MOURNER:
>The young tremble, his wisdom in their ears
>and so he journeys with us in his heart.

CHORUS:
>A triumph of manhood!

CHIEF MOURNER:
>The goddess waiting at the gate will meet
>a triumph of manhood.

IMOINDA: *(Feels the cloth)*
>Arrows of black and red. Black and red
>so befitting a Kromanti warrior.
>How like fresh blood this red is.
>O, father; such a man!
>*(Whispers to MAID)* I am found out.
>It is not true that I am fully a woman.
>I have such childish thoughts. *(Weeping)*
>I always wanted papa for myself,
>not shared, not shared with all our people.
>*(Falls into Esteizme's arms. She weeps; mourners wail).*
>Come, I am no stranger to death.
>Esteizme, have refreshments made ready
>for the mourners and the funeral party.

MAID:
> Yes, madam. First some water
> to wash the dust off their feet.

(Maid exits. Mourners surround Imoinda. Chief Mourner presents trophies. Tableau. Fade.)

MESSENGER:
> I must speak with mistress Imoinda.

MAID:
> Must? You must speak with my mistress? Be off.
> Relatives wait their turn; friends are waiting.
> Is it a job you want? We have no need
> of gardeners, builders, diviners.
> See how you force me to be uncivil.
> In this house it is a time of sorrow.

MESSENGER:
> What a tongue you have on you, o.
> I hope the lady does not have to live too close
> with you. If she were milk, you'd turn her sour.

MAID:
> Was a time you'd have your ears boxed for this.
> I say: watch your tongue
> in the house of the Lion of Kromanti.

MESSENGER:
> Let me speak with the madam.

MAID:
> First I will know your message.

MESSENGER: *(Aside)*
> I curse the day I ever was sent to this village.

MAID:
> I have no time for idle men's curses.
> *(Begins to walk away)*

MESSENGER:
> The Prince is on his way
> to visit the lady of the house, o.

MAID: *(Over her shoulder)*
> And which Prince is this?

MESSENGER:
> Which Prince? Prince Oko himself.
> We have no other. Eh!
> You can see I am a messenger
> from the royal household.

MAID:
> Oh! You took your time telling me this.
> And how is our fine and noble Prince Oko?

MESSENGER:
> They say the general died saving his life.
> Now the spirits lead him a dance about it.

MAID:
> When is not one thing is two.

MESSENGER:
> But it was like father and son, those two, o!
> They say the Prince was the son he never had.

MAID:
> Even so. Why listen for death?
> Don't mind me. Refreshment is served yonder.
> *(Takes him aside)*

Act One Scene 1

On no account must you speak to my mistress.
I will pass your message on in good time.
We never know how the spirits move her
these days.

Scene 2: Old Guinea.

At the edge of the forest beside Papa General's home. PRINCE OKO and his companion, overhearing IMOINDA and ESTEIZME, her maid, learn of the former's reluctance to meet the prince. PRINCE OKO finds himself attracted to IMOINDA. Enter Prince Oko and his companion, Baku. They carry their horses' tackle. MUSIC — "Journey That Counts" theme.

PRINCE OKO:

How much further, Baku?
Seems old Papa General
was dead right about you.
Full of wind, my old friend,
empty wind without rain.
I would no longer be friends
with your oaths for they are false.
Papa General was right.

You swore you knew this village.
Yet clearly you do not.
Take this upon your shoulder;
Carry your blame. It is yours.
I will waste no more time
in search of this maiden.
Seems old Papa General
was dead right about you.

BAKU:

"This maiden" is not just any maiden.
She's the only child of Papa General
former lion of our nation; your friend.

PRINCE OKO:

Come, we've tried. I'll send word to her instead.

BAKU:

> Sh! A village woman! More than one?
> Here's some chance of sport. *(Pulls OKO into bushes)*

IMOINDA:

> Like the swallow in flight
> *(MUSIC - "Journey That Counts")*
> *(Voice off)* I'll follow too. Go well.

MAID: *(Enters)*

> I give up! Madam, I refuse
> to take this vile humour any more.
> *(Sits on a stone. Imoinda enters)*
> You keep us out of doors too long.
> Remember, we expect visitors.

IMOINDA:

> I invited none.

MAID:

> Since when do we need our guests "invited"?
> Remember! The prince's messenger.

IMOINDA:

> At this time, I don't care for visitors.

MAID:

> This is no ordinary visitor.
> It is the prince himself.

IMOINDA:

> Prince? Prince? Are you obsessed with princes?
> He is my father's prince.
> He will not find my father here, will he?
> It's not me he wants. He needs not visit me;
> I am no general of war. I cannot offer

the excitement of battle or victory;
a chosen foe's head to carry on a pole.

MAID:
Madam, but it's Prince Oko,
your father's favourite.

IMOINDA:
Enough! I know that only too well.

MAID:
Did I ever tell you about a man
running away from his village?
Maybe even running from himself.
No matter. He had to cross a river. . .

IMOINDA:
Your eyes tell all. I don't need a story.

MAID:
Well, then, as you please. Shall we walk home,
since man, nor song nor story pleases you?
I have grain to grind. I shall be busy! *(Exit both)*

(Re-enters Prince Oko with his hand covering Baku's mouth)

PRINCE OKO:
Well! Well! Not exactly welcoming!

BAKU:
I would never have believed it possible.
Words stick in my throat. Such disrespect
in such a one who must know better!

PRINCE OKO:
> It seems she doesn't care for princes.

BAKU:
> But why did you stop my mouth?
> I wanted to confront her.
> I would have told her, shown her
> the duty owing to a prince.

PRINCE OKO:
> I saw in a dream it would be so.
> She feels bitterly that I live
> while her father, brave, generous man,
> loved so by all the people does not.

BAKU:
> Too kind my fine Prince. And no excuse.
> Creatures of the other sex must, at least,
> if nothing else, hold a civil tongue
> until to understanding they may come.

PRINCE OKO:
> Maybe we should turn back but . . .

BAKU:
> Turn back? First we demand proper respect.
> *(MUSIC — "Triumph of Manhood" theme)*

PRINCE OKO:
> There's part of me would rather carry
> respect for her father; his memory.

BAKU:
> Baba! Such a fine man of our nation.
> You would hardly know this was his daughter.

PRINCE OKO:
Now, no disrespect, you jackal,
or you dishonour the man.

BAKU:
Pardon, my Prince!

PRINCE OKO:
Life has lost so much of its flavour
with Papa General gone.
And to cap it all, my father wants peace
at any cost despite my counsel.
Have I stomach left for this visit?
Will she find a pole for me to carry
aloft some victim's head?
(MUSIC - "It's A Bad Omen" theme)

BAKU:
Perhaps it was an omen; we should not go.

PRINCE OKO:
Perhaps. What say you to hunting first?

BAKU:
The very thing. I hear the hippos
up river grow bigger than elephants.

PRINCE OKO:
What say you we show them to our spears?
(They laugh and embrace)
Yet, I'd like to hear her voice again.

BAKU:
Whose?

PRINCE OKO:
> The bird's singing in the trees back yonder.
> A dove I would say.

BAKU:
> So! Something new afoot? Of course.

PRINCE OKO:
> There was something about her voice,
> did you not think? *(Enters MESSENGER)*

MESSENGER:
> My Lord, Prince Oko, son of the Mighty,
> *(Prostrate on the ground)*
> fine cub of the great King of our nation,
> Magnificent One who . . .

PRINCE OKO:
> You may rise.

MESSENGER:
> The king sends word of his third task.
> He commands you escort at some speed
> the General's daughter to the Palace.

PRINCE OKO:
> Ha! A princely third task,
> unless I am mistaken.
> Repeat that message.

MESSENGER:
> The king commands you bring
> the General's daughter to the Palace.

PRINCE OKO:
>Thank you. A matter of no choice at all.
>This is out of our hands. *(To Baku)* No bad command.
>I mean, so much for our hunting. Pity.

BAKU:
>Can not this fellow escort the General's daughter?

PRINCE OKO:
>Sure! And you can answer to the King. Why not?

BAKU:
>A thousand pardons. His Majesty
>no doubt had good purpose to his command.

PRINCE OKO:
>Don't teach me my duty. Messenger,
>the King commands the lady be escorted?

MESSENGER:
>By you, oh Prince.

(Exit. MUSIC — "Triumph of Manhood" and "Omen" fades)

Scene 3: Imoinda's compound.

MAID:
> People say there is witchcraft on you.

IMOINDA:
> Do I care what people say?

CHORUS:
> Her mistress is not herself today
> (MUSIC — "Tasted Sorrow")
> not since the old lion was laid to rest
> returned to the earth; returned to the earth
> pierced in the eye by a single arrow.
> Poor child alone; she has eaten sorrow.
> Her constant companion is sorrow.

IMOINDA:
> Stay out of doors; sweep the courtyard.
> If anyone approaches say at once I am sick
> and send them on their way.
> (Exits)

MAID:
> Whatever she says. (Sweeping)

(Enter BAKU and PRINCE OKO)

BAKU: (Smites three times upon the doorpost)
> The Prince attends you. Be swift.

MAID: (Curtsying)
> My humble greetings to the Prince
> and your good self. This is an honour.

BAKU: *(Aside)*
> She warbles, my Lord.

PRINCE OKO:
> You mean she sings a different tune?
> There were two birds in the woods.
> Each sang a different tune.

MAID:
> My head is beginning to spin
> with birds and tunes. Is there a meaning
> that I should catch?

BAKU:
> Go catch mistress Imoinda!
> The King commands her to the palace.

MAID:
> Good Prince, my mistress is not so well.
> You see, since her father, the General . . .

BAKU:
> You babble, now, good woman.
> *(Enters Imoinda)*

IMOINDA: *(Curtsying)*
> Prince Oko, in my father's remembrance
> I greet you. *(To BAKU)* I would thank you
> to save your torments for some other place.

PRINCE OKO:
> Imoinda, since we last met
> you are so changed.

IMOINDA:
Time does that with no help from man
or woman, friend or foe and
even to princes, I understand.

PRINCE OKO:
Forgive me. I must stop gawping.
I remember you being quiet, a mere . . .

IMOINDA:
That was a long time ago.
The King commands you here?

PRINCE OKO:
No and yes. I was on my way
to share your sorrow, of course.
Please allow me that. Your father
was like a father to me. It is no secret.
Walk with me a little. *(They move aside)*
You are fully a woman.

IMOINDA:
As you are a man, prince Oko.

PRINCE OKO:
I don't know what I was expecting
when I first set out.

IMOINDA:
Nothing perhaps. And again, perhaps
off the battlefield, you find you don't know
what to expect. I know it happened
often to my father. After battle,
ordinary things seemed strange to him.

PRINCE OKO:
Don't be angry. I didn't want him killed.
He taught me so very much.
But you are a fine-spirited one, though.

IMOINDA:
Oh?

PRINCE OKO:
No, that's not it. You are very. . . . May I? *(Lifts her chin)*
You are beautiful. I didn't realise.

IMOINDA:
Is this something that the king commands?
Beauty masks a multitude of defects.
So, we do not value it too highly.
Besides, it fades.

PRINCE OKO:
I hope you will not be angry too long
with me. Give me your hand to friendship.
(Takes her hand)

IMOINDA:
And the King? *(Removes her hand)*

PRINCE OKO:
The King desires your presence at the Palace.
We celebrate peace with our neighbour
Chief Sitiangolu in the East.
So, I must escort you to the court.

IMOINDA:
Very well. If I may be excused.
Come, Esteizme. *(Both exit)*

PRINCE OKO:
> So few women have been in my life. Why?
> Let me breathe easy for it feels
> as if I have drunk greedily of palm wine.

BAKU:
> Your thirst was of your own making, sire.

PRINCE OKO: *(Sighs)*
> Women I've met before were not like her.
> I need a battle; enemies to face.

BAKU:
> What now?

PRINCE OKO:
> No better time. Besides, battle
> may be better for my heart. But she
> is cold. She doesn't care for me.

BAKU:
> No matter. If it is the King's command.

PRINCE OKO:
> It is not the King's command I want
> but rather her heart's command.
> What am I saying? I'm touched by the sun.
> There was a cool breeze all the while
> and now, I swear, it's stopped.
> *(MUSIC - "Omen" theme)*

BAKU:
> Is that so sire? I had not noticed.
> Good Prince, though you are wise,
> there is much you need to know of women.
> It is better always to have a woman
> who shows respect and knows her duty.

PRINCE OKO:
Page or tutor, which are you?

BAKU:
Page, tutor and friend, my lord.

PRINCE OKO:
Remember that. *(Sighs)* She has such fiery eyes,
such spirited ways.
Her skin at the tips of my fingers. Look!
What is happening to me?

BAKU:
My lord, you make a woman master
of your will! This is not as it should be.

PRINCE OKO:
Master? I must speak with her again. *(Knocks)*

MAID: *(Re-enters)*
She is not ready, sire.

PRINCE OKO:
(Enters IMOINDA. Exit MAID)
Just a word. You are still angry.
Really. I am deadly serious.
You cannot hate me because
your father loved me.
Think why he loved me.
Would he love so dearly
someone you would hate?
I give you my oath I would love you
however much you hated me.
Give me your hand to that.

IMOINDA:
    Prince Oko, what are you saying?
    I am confused.

PRINCE OKO:
    Give me your hand.

IMOINDA:
    Is that your command?

PRINCE OKO:
    I could command but it will not
    be the same. Give me your hand
    to our understanding.

IMOINDA:
    Which is?

PRINCE OKO:
    The more you hate me, I will love you more.
    So you will have to choose. Your hand?

(Stretches out a hand and waits. She offers hers. He takes it then lightly brushes her cheek. She pulls away)

BAKU: *(Breaking the spell)*
    My lord! The royal drummer!

PRINCE OKO:
    Royal drummer?

BAKU:
    Yes, if I may refresh your memory.
    (Aside to PRINCE OKO)
    Good Prince, there may be magic afoot here.

PRINCE OKO:
>It's in her eyes; it's in her eyes.
>When I look into her eyes; a doe's eyes,
>my soul takes fire
>and soars to reach the sky.
>Don't catch me
>let me rise until I fall again,
>*(MUSIC — "Enchanted Night")*
>don't catch me.
>
>When I touch her skin,
>so soft, and with such a sheen
>my fingertips glow.
>I want to trace a trail
>no snail will ever know,
>but just as slow a touch
>at least as slow.
>
>Is that magic? If so tell me.
>I haven't come across the like before.
>Is that magic?
>If so, then perhaps I should know.

BAKU:
>Madam, excuse us, if you will.
>The Prince is not so well, himself.
>I guess he has a touch of, um,
>battle fever. It happens.
>*(Exit both)*

IMOINDA:
>Esteizme! I am going to cry.
>*(ESTEIZME enters. Imoinda paces)*
>No, I'm going to laugh or do something
>very . . . I don't know, except that,
>usually I do know what I am going to do.
>Right?

MAID:
>Right.

IMOINDA:
>See how the leaves tremble.
>*(MUSIC - "Enchanted Night")*
>Was there ever such a night?
>Enchanted night
>stay always just so.
>I hear the trees.
>I can almost touch the sap.
>See the beads of life,
>hear the juices flowing.
>Tap, tap, tap!
>Hear the juices flowing.
>
>Zest in the air!
>No joke; no joke. *(MAID laughs)*
>It's true. Listen.
>I hear the trees'
>shimmying wings beat.
>See how the leaves tremble.

MAID: *(Laughs)*
>Yes. Yes. Just so. I see trembling.
>Not in the trees.
>Not in the leaves.
>Nor yet in your eyes.
>But if you'll allow me,
>It's in your heart. *(Places a hand on Imoinda's heart)*

IMOINDA:
>What is?

MAID:
>Enchantment. I am happy;
>you live again. And yet . . .

IMOINDA:

Not now. Do not start again to read
my future. I forbid it.
I am afraid enough already.
Afraid, I am bewitched.

(Re-enters PRINCE OKO; exit MAID)

PRINCE OKO:

Tell me, Imoinda.
Do you feel the same way?
(Brushes her cheek and lifts up her chin)

IMOINDA:

I can almost touch the sap *(MUSIC — "Bad Omen")*
See the beads of life
hear the juices flowing.
Tap, tap, tap!
Hear the juices flowing.

PRINCE OKO:

I shall speak with my father, the King.

IMOINDA:

I don't know what to say.

PRINCE OKO:

Then say nothing. I'll speak with my father.
Three tasks he has given me and then
there will be time to speak with him.

IMOINDA:

We have surely no need to rush.

PRINCE OKO:

Have we not? Wish I had rushed here sooner.
I command you get your things.
The drummer is at the gate.
Let me deliver you to the Palace
and then when all is gathered there,
conduct the Chief, our once enemy
safely through the nation,
to be centre of the celebration.

BAKU:

It is a bad omen
a bad omen *(SONG - "Bad Omen")*
when a Prince of this nation
becomes so enchanted.

What if the battle horn
sounds right now?
What if the oracle says

not so; not now?
Then what will become
of it all? *(Exit IMOINDA)*

PRINCE OKO:

Why do you stand there looking like doom?

BAKU:

We must make haste to the fetish priest.

PRINCE OKO:

For you?

BAKU:

No, good Prince. You see, while a Prince
can always choose a wife, the one thing

he must avoid is enchantment.
You have fallen foul of this, my lord.

PRINCE OKO:
I shall look for the charms and potions
of which you speak in my lady's eyes.

BAKU:
You may mock, but *(Enter IMOINDA and MAID)*
it is a bad omen.

MAID:
She smiles again, what joy
(MUSIC — "Enchanted Night")
like after heavy rain, the sun.

PRINCE OKO:
To the Palace. And with my tasks complete,
I get to feast my eyes the more on you.

IMOINDA:
How should I know when these tasks are done?
Am I to grow grey hairs waiting?

PRINCE OKO:
Not so long. Only let your maid watch
where I hang my harness and my quiver.
When next I hang them up, find me there.

(They join the drummer and procession at the gate. Exit)

Scene 4. At the Palace.

The KING entertains his neighbouring CHIEF and rival. In the Palace garden where OKO's harness and quiver hang, two teams play out a tug of war. MUSIC — "Triumph of Manhood". CHIEF crosses to harness then exits. IMOINDA crosses. She traces patterns with her fingers on OKO's harness.

IMOINDA:
>Day dreaming, day dreaming
>*(SONG — "Day Dreaming")*
>standing here all on my own
>just day dreaming
>dreaming the whole day through
>about the man I long
>to have beside me;
>dreaming the whole day through
>about the man I long to see.
>*(Enters PRINCE OKO)*
>His hands they touch me so.
>His voice. *(Sighs)* I tremble.
>Is he so very tall?
>I don't even care at all.
>His eyes, let me see,
>they drink me up
>almost to the very last drop.
>Day, dreaming, day dreaming.

PRINCE OKO:
>Your maid keeps good watch.

IMOINDA:
>You made me jump! Yes, she watches well.
>But, I doubt hers are the only eyes.
>And your tasks are they complete my lord ?

PRINCE OKO:
>Now the festivities can begin
>for the grand peace my father plans.
>One task remains and that must be
>tonight while sleep caresses you.
>Then shall I have claimed my father's ears.

IMOINDA:
>You wear a good many fetishes.

PRINCE OKO:
>All prescribed at Baku's insistence
>to protect me from your magic.
>I confess, though I will not tell him so,
>your magic is too potent. I am dust
>in a lusty wind even as I stand
>quietly before you, Imoinda.

IMOINDA:
>No less am I before you. Perhaps
>I too need the fetish's prescription.
>*(MUSIC — "Enchanted Night")*

PRINCE OKO:
>No, not so. I hear the diviner's voice.
>Listen. He says,
>"being with each other is the cure". *(They laugh)*
>Look, what do you say to this likeness?
>*(Holds a small carving)*

IMOINDA:
>Who fashioned it? You?

PRINCE OKO:
>I cannot blame anyone else.

IMOINDA:
    Ah! Wait! How does this compare?
    (Takes a small carving from her wrap)

PRINCE OKO:
    Did you fashion this?
    (MUSIC - "Bad Omen". Enters CHIEF)

IMOINDA:
    No other. Would I have dared ask
    another to fashion your likeness for me
    and risk loose tongues and common ridicule?

PRINCE OKO:
    Imoinda, the likeness is so fine.
    Let's exchange; I'll wear yours and you wear mine
    until we hear my father's words.
    Luck looks certain to be ours.
    Besides, it is a new moon tonight.

IMOINDA:
    And what might the new moon mean?

PRINCE OKO:
    It means that I must go hunting
    on my father's business: the King's business.
    Till this is done, it is impossible
    to claim a moment with him.
    So, I am impatient to be gone,
    the sooner to claim you. Help me.

IMOINDA:
    How?

PRINCE OKO:
>Go now and I to the final task.
>*(MUSIC — "Enchanted Night". The lovers exit. Exit CHIEF who has observed them)*

In another part of the palace. A ritual wrestling bout is in progress. The King and Chief are seated side by side watching the performance enacting their former struggles.

KING:
>Just so we two were.

CHIEF:
>First one is vanquished, then the other.

KING:
>Till at last we knew our might was even.
>*(The wrestlers lean against each other to stay upright)*

CHIEF:
>Generals died to prove it was not so.

KING: *(Calling)*
>Stop the fight. Bring out the cloak of peace.
>You know our pride. Forward the tug of war!

CHORUS:
>Stop the fight. Bring out the cloak of peace.

KING:
>Our dynasty has cloaked few enemies.
>But you, our neighbour Chief deserves this.
>*(Pours libation)*

CHORUS:
>Spirits of our ancestors, peace we call;
>spirits of our ancestors, peace.

Between the giving and receiving
fill this cloak with peace that lasts.

CHIEF:
My friend we drink to peace. Thanks for this cloak.
May it ever fit, as long as we live.

KING:
Wear it well. Our new lion, my son
has gone to the hunt. As is our custom,
the pelt he brings back claims honour.

CHORUS:
Honour sits tonight on your right shoulder.

CHIEF:
Ah! A proud father. You deserved more sons.
In my line are sons to fill a grain store.
You must bear more; take care of your new wife,
my daughter. Treat her well, your youngest wife.

CHORUS:
She will give you sons to match your manhood.

KING:
Yes, yes. And now to the crowning matter.
Of my daughters, the princesses,
tell me the substance of your choosing.

CHIEF:
My friend, it's so hard. So many daughters.
Each time I think I choose, there's another.

KING:
What? Have two! Have more!

CHIEF:

> My friend, I passed her in the garden and
> she is the one you have not introduced.
> Why? Are you keeping her for someone else?

KING:

> Never. You honour me to take my daughter.
> Any maiden in this Palace is yours.
> I have promised none to any other.
> Whom you choose, you wed. That is my word.

CHORUS:

> The King's bond; his final solemn word.

CHIEF:

> We drink to your word! I speak of she
> who came back to the Palace with your son.

KING:

> Now who can that be? Messenger!

(Enters MESSENGER. They whisper. He exits and re-appears with Imoinda)

KING:

> My daughter, I have not greeted you.

CHIEF:

> A comely daughter.

KING:

> Daughter of the Lion of Kromanti,
> Arise! I have truly neglected you. *(Pours libation)*
> May the ancestors heap their blessing
> upon this deed. *(To Imoinda)* The title of Princess
> I confer on you by special decree
> and land, cattle and cowries as fitting.

Don't thank me. In time you'll know better
whom you owe this much. Now, leave us.

(Exits Imoinda).

CHIEF:
Do you think ill of me for choosing
the daughter of your valiant general?
Or would you marry her yourself?

KING:
If you will have her as our daughter,
here's my hand. She is yours.
I have promised her to no-one else.

CHORUS:
On the King's honour, the woman is yours.

Scene 5: Another part of the Palace.
IMOINDA enters from the bridal bath. She is being dressed by her MAID. MUSIC — "Something Doesn't Fit".

MAID:
>Summoned to the bridal bath so soon?
>Your prince makes, I swear, too quick a groom.

IMOINDA:
>So it seems.

MAID:
>Stretch out your arms. "So it seems!"
>Tonight your skin will be oiled till it gleams.

IMOINDA:
>I am afraid. Something's not quite right.
>*(Knocking at the door)*

MESSENGER:
>His Excellency and our honoured guest
>await the Princess Imoinda.

IMOINDA: *(To MAID)*
>Go at once, ask if the Prince has returned.

MAID:
>What difference does that make?
>*(Knocking at the door)*

IMOINDA:
>Go! *(MUSIC — "Bad Omen". Exit MAID)*
>A dark veil stretched across the moon. No!
>Sometimes there is in the look of someone
>a veil of a thing, a something

that makes you think, I must not trust you
or, that there lurks beneath the veil
something dangerous; something waiting.

MAID:
> *(Re-enters)*
> No, good Princess, the Prince is not returned.

IMOINDA:
> What can this mean? The King and Chief
> were whispering when I was summoned
> to the chamber earlier. And oh his look!

MAID:
> Whose look? Ah, the Chief has things on his mind.
> He will choose one of the princesses.

IMOINDA:
> Am I not now a princess of this land?
> *(Knocking again)*

MAID:
> The King's daughters are very many!
> Hurry! We must to the King with all speed!

IMOINDA :
> Suppose . . . *(MUSIC — "Triumph of Manhood")*

MAID:
> Suppose I tell you what I see before me?
> You look so beautiful.
> Your father would have been so proud
> to see you betrothed to no less a one
> than his very favourite.

IMOINDA:
My heart.

MAID:
Of course. So it should be.

IMOINDA:
Something doesn't fit. I tell you;
Something doesn't fit, I say.
(MUSIC — "Something Doesn't Fit")

MAID:
Something doesn't fit, and yet
she deserves the kind of peace
any ordinary woman can get.

IMOINDA:
Why the knocking? What's the hurry?
The Prince cannot take me, if he is not here.

BOTH:
Something doesn't fit, I tell you,
something doesn't fit.
Can't place a finger
straight upon it. *(Knocking)*

IMOINDA:
I go in there. I think of Prince Oko
and he is my prince, no harm will come.
I follow my heart what harm can come?
Surely, I deserve some small happiness.
(Throws the door open. Exits)

Scene 6:

Light drumming as maidens adjust masks. Backs to audience. Rhythmic clapping. Enter the KING and CHIEF. They are seated and given each a horn of drink.

MESSENGER:
> The masked dance of the bridal veil!

KING:
> With a bride we seal our alliance. *(Raising his horn)*
> With a bride we seal our fate.

CHORUS:
> Take a bride, clinch our deal, seal our fate.
> On with the dance; on with the dance.
> We've waited enough; seal our alliance.

CHIEF:
> Honour and triumph! On with the dance!
> *(Aside)* With this bride I claim my dominance,
> *(SONG — "On With The Dance")*
> this bride who carries a kingdom so vast.

KING:
> Take this bride; clinch our deal, seal our fate.

CHIEF:
> Trust me, believe me, I seal our fate.
> Her prince out of sight, I taste dominance.

CHORUS:
> On with the dance, on with the dance. *(Group dance)*
> We've waited enough; seal our alliance.

IMOINDA:
> Chosen One, I dance for you
> like the leaf does for the wind.
> Your tune, your tune alone calls to me.
> (Group dance)

MAID:
> Here's the rub. Can a woman choose?
> A woman choose? Taboo, taboo.
> Imoinda, truly I fear for you.
> Our women don't choose; must not choose.

CHORUS:
> Taboo, taboo, taboo, taboo. (MUSIC — "Bad Omen")
> Men choose for honour; only men choose.
> What happens when you break the taboo?
> Taboo, taboo, taboo, taboo.

CHIEF:
> Enough! I choose my bride! (IMOINDA is veiled)

KING:
> Remove your masks!
> (Signals and dancers exit except MAID. IMOINDA's feet are sprinkled with blood and herbs)
> You, look to your mistress!

IMOINDA:
> Your Highest Excellency! (Imoinda prostrates herself)

MAID:
> (Whispers) Mercy! (To IMOINDA) Speak!

IMOINDA:
> I am already betrothed, your majesty.
> (MUSIC — "Enchanted Night")

KING:

> Silence! On pain of death to any man
> whose name you'd choose to mention at this time.

CHIEF:

> I take no offence; let her make ready.
> and I'll send a few gifts to her quarters.
> *(KING signals. IMOINDA and MAID exit)*
> They say the more reluctant the bride,
> the sweeter the nuptials! *(They drink)*

CHORUS:

> Take this bride; clinch our deal, seal our fate.
> Trust me, believe me, We seal our fate.

CHIEF:

> Her prince out of sight, I taste dominance.

BOTH:

> Honour and triumph! On with the dance.
> We've waited enough; I taste dominance.
> *(As they both dance, enter PRINCE OKO and BAKU)*

PRINCE OKO:

> Royal Father, honoured guest.
> What a night of hunting!
> *(Throws a pelt upon the table and a scroll)*

KING:

> Aha! My son's honour is fully restored.

BAKU:

> I crave your indulgence please, my liege.
> Press, first, your royal eyelids together.
> Now open wide your eyes and behold!

Step this way, step high, Prince Oroonoko.
(*MUSIC — "First Bride"*)
Step this way Man-Prince who is ready.
He is ready to claim his first bride.

It's no easy task to train a prince.
So I take pride in this prince among men,
a prince among flesh who has chosen.

CHIEF: *(Drinks)*
There is something in the air this night.

PRINCE OKO:
I claim my first bride, Imoinda. *(Kneeling)*
No maiden I have seen compares with her.
Such a match; lion meets his lioness.
A match decreed by the heavens, no less.
I claim my first bride, Imoinda!

KING:
Silence! Not another sound.
Imoinda is betrothed this night
to our esteemed guest.

PRINCE OKO:
What? This cannot be.

KING:
I am afraid, so it is.

CHIEF:
Ah! My friend, I have many daughters.
You can have one for each night.

BAKU:
Why, that is most fortunate. *(MUSIC — "Bad Omen")*

PRINCE OKO:
> I have no interest in your daughters.
> Baku, I command you, communicate
> to the King and his honoured guest
> every detail of which we have just learnt.

BAKU:
> Sire, as we travelled back . . .

PRINCE OKO:
> Let the palm wine flow. *(To MESSENGER)*
> See to it personally that the Chief's horn is never empty.
> *(To Baku)* The map. *(Upturns table. Exits)*

KING:
> I'll teach that whelp. He was ever too impulsive.

CHIEF:
> Tomorrow, he will feel better.

BAKU:
> Sire, the map! And our security!
> Seems many flying canoes have landed
> upon the coast. They make trade in our people
> and take them as slaves across the waters.

KING:
> What do you mean "our people"?

CHIEF:
> I have heard some matter like this before.

BAKU:
> There was a trader waiting at the gate.
> Shall I have him attend your Majesty?

KING:
>No! This night was for our celebration.
>Where is our only Prince of the nation?

CHIEF:
>First a guard for my bride's compound.
>Now, tell all. *(Lights fade)*

Scene 7: Imoinda's guest chamber.

PRINCE OKO: *(Tapping on the door and calling softly)*
 Imoinda! *(MUSIC — "Enchanted Night")*

MAID:
 (Going to the door) Too late!

PRINCE OKO:
 Let me in.

IMOINDA:
 Open the door. *(Enters PRINCE OKO)* Leave us.

MAID:
 Madam. I dare not.

PRINCE OKO:
 I command you. *(Exits MAID)* Imoinda, will you marry
 Sitiangolu?

IMOINDA:
 There is death upon your head
 should I call out your name.

PRINCE OKO:
 This carving I gave is sign enough
 of our betrothal.
 As I rode back from the forest,
 the new moon guiding the way,
 my thoughts ran always to you, my bride.
 The moon will be our witness; you're my bride.
 (Lights fade)

PRINCE OKO:
 Let the moon light on our act of oneness
 (SONG — "We Are One")

softly polish your body as we touch.
Mould your form into mine; we are one.

BOTH:
Moon, moon mark our bodies as we touch;
with the stars be our witness, we are one.

PRINCE OKO:
Imoinda we have nothing to hide.

IMOINDA:
My Prince Oroonoko, we have nothing to hide.

BOTH:
Moon, moon mould our bodies as we touch.
With the stars be our witness. We are one.

PRINCE OKO:
One knocking heart; one body. We are one.

IMOINDA:
One knocking heart; one body. We are one.

BOTH:
With the stars be our witness; we are one.
("Moon Witness")

(Lights fade. MUSIC. A knocking grows louder)

CHIEF:
(Voice calls drunkenly) Woman! Open the door. I have
come to take you, my bride.

IMOINDA:
Oroonoko!

PRINCE OKO:

> I shall dispatch him once and for all. *(Opens the door)*
> Who is this would disturb my bride
> with such foul noise and even fouler breath?

CHIEF:

> A light! *(Chief falls upon OKO's neck)*

PRINCE OKO:

> Light here for the likes of you?
> And in such a state? Get him to a bed! *(Closes door)*

CHIEF:

> Guards! Murder! Robbery! Fetch the king!
> *(Cries and commotion)*

KING: *(Enters)*

> Is there to be no peace this night? Lights!
> *(Chief whispers to the King)*
> Prince Oko, is that you? What means you?
> Speak or you tempt my sword.
> *(MUSIC — "She Has Tasted Sorrow")*

PRINCE OKO:

> It is customary, my liege, *(At the door)*
> for a man to sleep with his bride in peace.

CHIEF:

> Such disrespect merits war! Revenge!

PRINCE OKO:

> And we'll fight. No man of this nation
> is afraid of war. We'll fight. *(Enters MAID)*

CHIEF:

> I claim retribution for my honour!

KING:

Seize them! Unspeakable dishonour
to my name, this dynasty and this nation! *(Oko resists)*
Bind him! He is not my son! *(MUSIC up)*
You, madam, shall be food for crocodiles.

CHIEF:

The trader at the gate shall have this slave.
I'll have no less a price as I am a man.

PRINCE OKO:

Father, let me yet command our men!

KING:

Hold your tongue! Guards, lay hands on him.
Never again to darken this palace.
You, too, once princess! To the slave trader
and let him be gone on the instant. *(Indicates MAID)*
Take this witch also. She offends my sight.
(They are led off)
I've reached that point now of no turning back.

CHORUS:

Out of reach. Peace he'd hoped for
out of reach. In our time, out of reach.

KING:

My luck, my fate sealed.
First my friend, my trusted general gone;
Now my son, my only heir. What have I done?
(Gong sounds)
(MUSIC — "Tasted Sorrow")

Scene 8: Outside The Palace gate.
IMOINDA wears a long wooden yoke.

IMOINDA:
>If you see me broken, lonesome, walk by.
>Don't stop to ask a question. Though
>
>you may have glimpsed my face before
>I am no more a maiden of this land.
>
>An orphan woman stands before you.
>No home for me now, but save your pity.
>
>While you fix your gaze upon my necklace
>I'll be searching for my lover's eyes.
>*(IMOINDA is moved on, Enters PRINCE OKO, bound)*

PRINCE OKO:
>Imoinda!
>Fear not, my own dove, for I follow.
>No matter my feet are shackled like this.
>Imoinda!
>
>These hands now bound with sinews
>have seen battles more than you've known moons,
>have slain enemies more than you could guess.
>Enemies come; they go. Where are they all?
>
>Imoinda!
>Trust me; times will change. With you beside me,
>fortune will smile once more upon us.
>Imoinda!

ACT TWO
Nightmare Canoe

Scene 1
On board a slaveship, "The Greenwich". Bales stacked ship shape. Dim lights. Wooden structure. Lanterns swing with the rocking, creaking, groaning of the slaveship. Shackled bodies on the bales come partly into the glare of the lanterns and then recede. Whipcrack. IMOINDA stumbles and falls into an open space among the bales. SAILOR ties her to a post.

CHORUS:
> Nightmare canoe! Canoe! Hold on!

SAILOR:
> Won't eat? Can't eat? Lucky to eat at all. Then agen, this'll whet your appetite, I expect. Them don't call me "strip em whip em" for nothen.

(Tears at Imoinda's cloth. The shadow of the whip falls. Female figures fill the shadows. Last is ESTEIZME. Women block her reaching Imoinda. Struggle. Rumble of pain and song)

CHORUS :
> Nightmare canoe! Canoe!

SAILOR: *(Cracking the whip)*
> That's starters then, by Captain's orders. So, which nigger's goin' to teach her what to do wi' good food on the *Greenwich*?

(ESTEIZME is allowed through. She takes up the calabash of food).

IMOINDA:
>I sleep? I dream? Or I'm dead? You too?
>*(Low humming)*

ESTEIZME
>Eat.

IMOINDA:
>To be punished like this, I have done wrong.

ESTEIZME
>Eat! The gods of our ancestors will tell.

IMOINDA:
>Taboo. It is the taboo I have broken.
>I must die. Look how I have changed the world!
>
>I have caused unspeakable demons
>with so many instruments of torture
>to rise and escape from the bush of ghosts

ESTEIZME
>Imoinda, such power is not yours.
>Trust me, one who has watched over you.

CHORUS:
>Nightmare canoe! Canoe! Hold on!

IMOINDA:
>Who are these? My eyes search everywhere.
>Prince Oko! I long to see you; touch you.
>*(Whipcrack)*
>Look how your name angers even pale gods.
>Oroonoko! Your name is such sorrow.

Act Two Scene 1

ESTEIZME:
>Eat! Our new family awaits you.
>Shipmates all; our family in sorrow.

CHORUS:
>Nightmare canoe! Canoe! Hold on for the children.

IMOINDA:
>What children?

ESTEIZME: *(Handing over the calabash)*
>The children on board who share our fate.

CHORUS: *(Whipcrack)*
>Nightmare canoe! Canoe! Hold on! *(Imoinda eats)*

Orders of "Clear the deck". OKO in chains is picked out by a moving beam of light as he is flung into the space. Swinging beams/ angled spotlights.

OKO:
>Can't see. Can't see through this nightmare.
>*(SONG — "Nightmare Canoe")*

CHORUS:
>Nightmare canoe, canoe. Nightmare canoe.

OKO:
>I feel the stranglehold of darkness
>deeper than the heart of a forest.
>*(Wailing and whiplash echo)*

CHORUS:
>Nightmare canoe, canoe. Canoe.

OKO:

> Listen! Echoes warn of evil:
> Man against man, against woman and child.

CHORUS:

> Nightmare canoe, canoe. Nightmare canoe.

OKO:

> Answering echoes line this filthy cave
> ooze stench like rotting corpses in the sun.

CHORUS:

> Nightmare canoe, canoe. Nightmare canoe.

OKO:

> What place is this? How is it to be named?

CHORUS:

> It's called a ship of slaves, of fools, of thieves
> but we say, a nightmare canoe, canoe.

OKO:

> I demand to speak with your general.
> I will not stay. I say again, I am a Prince.

SAILOR:

> What he shouting about now?

VOICE:

> Says him be Prince.

SAILOR:

> An' I be king of the baboons. Right bleedin lot we got
> this trip. Roll on Barbadoes. Then roll on Deptford.
> You, fella! Got a lesson coming to you. Nobody makes
> the boatswain's mate eat two of his own front teeth

and gets away with it. If you ain't seen hell afore today, remember, "strip em, whip em" showed you hell.

(Light shows men in chains assembled. The back of a uniformed figure points a hunting gun. Chorus of chains and humming. Oko is whipped in silence. SAILOR exits. OKO roars his anger into the wind. "My Imoinda" MUSIC fade. Spotlight on IMOINDA. "Heart Drum" MUSIC).

IMOINDA:
> Heart drum. Heart drum. Hush.
> *(MUSIC — "Enchanted Night")*
> Hush or explode. Can one body bear more?
> Heart drum, heart drum hush.
> Sound mocks me. Silence is a new friend now.
> Heart drum hush, lie still, hush up
> unless, unless you are the talking drum,
> silent messenger from a world known once
> now struck dumb, dumbstruck by cold misfortune.

OKO:
> Heart drum. Heart drum. Hush
> Hush or explode. Can one body bear more?
> Sound mocks me. Silence is a new friend now.
> Silence is a drumbeat, so faint
> you cannot hear, a single wing beat
> strain all you might, you cannot hear.
> Heart drum, hush. Silence is my friend.

(Lights fade. Spotlight on ESTEIZME another part of the ship. "I Had Almost Forgot" MUSIC.)

ESTEIZME:
(SONG — "I Had Almost Forgot")
> Once when still a little girl, so high
> a wise woman walked into our village

each of her eyes had a blue ring to it.
She took me, "the serious one" she called me,
to serve with her at the mountain peak
where the air is cool and blue and still.
I had almost forgot.

CHORUS:
And should not all the world go bad
when the priestess herself forgets her role?
Yes the world goes rotten. The stench is here.

ESTEIZME:
She taught me how to search answers out
in a clear pool or a calabash
at the shrines of our gods, our ancestors,
how to gain a god's ear and how listen.
The hardest of all is to listen
for answers are mostly well hidden
and I had almost forgotten.

CHORUS:
Then should not all the world go bad
when the priestess herself forgets her role?
Yes, the world goes rotten. The stench is here.

ESTEIZME:
To hear answers in the wind, in the leaves,
in the patterning of birds in flight,
in the scurrying of ants in single file.
Soon my service became serving you and
the Wise One said one day I'd come to know
such that she could not even name.
I had almost forgotten.

CHORUS:
And should not all the world go bad?

Yes, the world goes rotten. The stench is here.
You can smell it; taste it for yourself.

OKO:
>Silence is a drumbeat.
>Dumb sound take a message to my father.
>Hollow sound empty like a dry wind;
>empty like the stomach after bile.

CHORUS:
>Lash! Feel the rhythm! Lash! Feel the rhythm!

OKO:
>What drum is this? Who makes my back a drum?
>Dumb sound take a message to my father.
>You talking drum that once was my back
>take a message from a lost son to a king.
>Say silence is a drumbeat echoing,
>silence is the sting of skin on my skin.
>Who can ever cure this drum skin
>that once was my back?

SAILOR:
>Says he be a prince. Got airs and graces to fit. What?
>Tell the Captain? Want me to be a laughing stock?
>Boatswain, Sir? I'm on me way, sir! There's Guinea gold
>in it! Well, Guinea gold will look as good in Deptford
>as in a Capn's chest! There's an end to the matter. So
>long as some trickles down my way. Blessed Mary, how
>the "*Greenwich*" groans and rolls!
>*(Crash of waves and creaking wood)*

VOICES:
>A hand! A hand! Make tight! Batten down! Seal the
>hatch! All hands on deck!
>*(Women huddle, wailing as waves crash, winds howl)*

CHORUS:
>Tossed and dashed and tossed again.
>Some new terror strikes the nightmare canoe.
>Hark! Hark! Lashing and roaring.
>Some new terror strikes the nightmare canoe.
>
>Prepare to fly! Perhaps the sides will crack
>Fly away! Fly away! We'll walk on back.
>Dreams come cheap in this nightmare canoe.
>We're trapped in this hole; nothing we can do.

ESTEIZME:
>No! Always, there is something we can do.

CHORUS:
>Hark! Hark! Lashing and roaring
>Some new terror strikes the nightmare canoe.
>Fly! Fly to the bottom of the sea.
>Find the portal back to old Guinea.

IMOINDA:
>Forgotten who you are? She speaks true.
>What we remember, the whip can't undo.

CHORUS:
>(SONG — "Number Eighty Three")
>I'm number eighty three. Best to forget.
>Raped again yesterday. Mouth stuffed with rope.
>(Spits)
>Tossed and dashed and tossed again,
>some new terror strikes the nightmare canoe.
>(Sounds of the ship)
>Come! Don't let those tears fall inside of you.
>We have each other for now and that's true.

IMOINDA:
> Number one, six, nine they refer to me.
> I was a young one betrothed to marry,
> youngest girl of seven, favourite of all.
> I long to see the face of my mammy.

CHORUS:
> Poor child alone, a friend stands beside you.
> We have each other for now and that's true.

ESTEIZME
> Take courage! See how we weather the storm.

IMOINDA:
> To be sure even a nightmare canoe
> must wash us up some place, some day. Courage!
> And should anyone gain the chance, send word
> to the children, and the menfolk, our brothers.

ESTEIZME:
> Yes. Always, there is something we can do.
> Remember and this will see us through.

IMOINDA:
> Can't forget who we are; she speaks true.
> What we remember, the whip can't undo.
> *(Thunder clap)*

VOICE:
> Man overboard! And another!
> Stop the bastards! We'll be ruined!

CHORUS:
> Hark! Hark! Lashing and roaring.
> Some new terror strikes the nightmare canoe.

Act Two Scene 1

(Spotlight on ESTEIZME and IMOINDA "Nightmare Canoe" MUSIC)

IMOINDA:

> When I close my eyes just so; not too tight;
> with just about the right amount of light,
> out of the darkness, I make out his face.
> Hush, I'll conjure him up just once more.
> So, if I never feel his warmth again;
> his fingers sending such sweet messages,
> doesn't matter. Watch my eyes; not too tight;
> with just about the right amount of light.

ESTEIZME:

> How can you say never? There are others
> who suffer. Besides, Prince Oko is here. Alive.

IMOINDA:

> Alive? You would not be so cruel!
> Here? What mixed blessing this is!
> Whoever we are; these words speak true.
> What we remember, the whip can't undo.

(A rumble of humming interspersed with "Hold on!" Lights fade)

Scene 2: Off ship.

MUSIC — "New Land". Conch. Outside the slave auction room and among a batch of slaves, IMOINDA waits in a penned area. All are oiled, fed and clothed in readiness for the sale. Already purchased, Oko sees Imoinda as he is led out. His new master watches the looks exchanged.

CHORUS:
>We walked big forest.
>Woy!
>We paddled long down river.
>Woy!
>We slept nights in pens.
>Woy!
>Then walked some more.
>Woy!
>We crossed big waters.
>Woy!
>We suffered chains and whips.
>What more for we to see?
>Woy!
>What more for we to see?
>Woy! Oh! Yoy!

DRIVER: *(Cracking a long whip)*
>Okay! Okay!
>Gentleman come fuh buy you. Now!
>*(MUSIC: — "Come Fuh Buy")*
>Look sharp! Straight back! Show dem teeth.
>*(Cracks whip)*
>Longer you stay in here, worse for you! *(Cracks whip)*
>Okay! Okay! Make way!

PLANTER:
>Driver, have my lot led out.
>Really, this is no place for gentlemen!

DRIVER: *(Cracking whip)*
>Yes, massa boss! Okay! Okay!
>Best slave lot for Woodlands plantation!
>Okay! Okay! Make way!

OROONOKO: *(Enters)*
>What land is this?
>I cannot tell whether the battle's lost
>or else I should persist.
>An army before me. No leader.
>What land is this?

IMOINDA:
>*(Pushes her way forward)* Prince Oroonoko!

PLANTER:
>He really is a comely slave.
>A prince of slaves. Can there be such a thing?
>I think I'll call him Caesar. Yes, Caesar!

IMOINDA:
>Oroonoko!
>See how the leaves tremble!
>I dream again! I dream again!

OROONOKO:
>Imoinda!
>*(Reaches for IMOINDA. DRIVER cracks the whip)*

PLANTER:
>Caesar! What is this I see before me?
>Is our Caesar now Mark Anthony?
>I believe he's found his Cleopatra!
>Ha! Ha! Ha!

>Stay your hand you slave of a dog.
>Let them be! Let them be!

Since I must tarry, here's new sport for me.
Ha! Ha! Ha!

I'll have the two and observe their story.
Add the slave woman to the bill of sale.
Meantime, I'll stick with Caesar
though he may prove himself Mark Anthony.
Ha! Ha! Ha!

DRIVER: *(Cracking a long whip)*
Okay! Okay!
Gentleman come fuh buy you. Now!
Look sharp! Straight back! Show dem teeth.
Longer you stay in here, worse for you!
Okay! Okay! Make way!

OROONOKO:
Imoinda! I am dreaming, too.
Just when I thought all was lost, I find you —
pinch me, whip me, even — I find you.

CHORUS:
Oroonoko! A prince of our land!
Oroonoko!
Warrior beyond the big mountain.
Oroonoko!

OROONOKO:
No. Without a father, I am no son.
If I can hold my Imoinda's hand,
I am a happy man again.

PLANTER:
Caesar! A man might indulge a slave
but only just so much and no more.
Come! To the plantation. To Woodlands.

ESTEIZME: *(Falls upon her knees)*
    I beg you master
    Do not separate me from my sister.
    I beg you. You'll have no regrets.
    (Clings to Planter's feet. Humming.)

DRIVER:
    Massa, give the word and I'll whip am!
    Sides, big boss massa would na like it.
    You get too many new slaves.

PLANTER:
    "Big boss massa would na like it?"
    Then, I like it pretty damn well!
    The ship's papers — let me inspect them.

DRIVER: *(Knocking on back door)*
    Ship's papers for massa!

PLANTER:
    Males adult: one hundred and fifteen.
    Females adult: eight six.
    Boys: ninety eight.
    Girls: sixty one.
    By my sums, that makes a mighty number.
    One more slave can hardly be noticed.

(Esteizme is purchased. Planter and slaves process out. Lights fade. The hammer falls. Auctioneer's voice)

VOICE:
    What am I bid? What am I bid?
    Newly arrived from Guinea
    and seasoned to our clime.
    Parcel one: six boys, three males,
    one girl, one adult female.
    What am I bid? What am I bid?

ACT THREE
Burden And Birth

Scene 1: On the plantation
*Work song dies as slaves disperse at dusk. OKO falls in with
ESTEIZME in the direction of the Great House.*

OKO:
>That Pincher has voice to carry a man's heart.

ESTEIZME:
>Uh-huh.

OKO:
>To carry even its secret beating.

ESTEIZME:
>Uh-huh.

OKO:
>Though I've seen her only from afar
>since we landed here, I won't complain.

ESTEIZME:
>You have a secret to deliver?

OKO:
>If only it would find her.

ESTEIZME:
>Tell me and Pincher will set it to song.
>Musicians travel, so might a message.

OKO:
>Tell her my heart is heavy
>when she is so far away.

I thought that here at last
she would be my wife.
It is still not so.

ESTEIZME:
Your heart is heavy.

OKO:
Tell her my eyes are clouded
when she is so far away.
I thought that here at last
she would be my wife.
It is still not so.

ESTEIZME:
Your eyes see dimly.

OKO:
Tell her she'll find her lion
waiting for the mate he chose.

DRIVER: *(Enters)*
What you doing here?
Late again from the field. Stocks, tonight!

OKO:
I must speak with massa boss.

DRIVER:
This not nigger quarters. This out of bounds.
Stocks out yonder and extra whipping
will learn you.

OKO:
I must speak with massa boss.

DRIVER:

> Every night you hangin round.
> This night the whip'll find you
> before moonlight catch your tail afire
> or else massa's musket and powder
> leave such a hole no hand can patch.

OKO:

> I do not fear implements of war.
> I am ... I was.

DRIVER:

> Yes, you was! I know. I met you before.

OKO:

> We met before? Explain yourself.

DRIVER: *(Laughs)*

> I mean times change. Look we now!
> You could no guess under Guinea's sun
> how times would change us.

OKO:

> By the sacred memory of Guinea ...

DRIVER:

> Guinea is only dream. Gone. Forgotten.
> Here I stay a chameleon. Different skin.

OKO:

> A dog does not change its skin.

DRIVER:

> Twice a dog? You must taste my bite!

OKO:

    I must speak with massa boss.

DRIVER:

    Your massa Boss gone fo married.
    Then, your massa Boss gone in big ship.
    First, you better speak with me.
    In this land, eh, one-time prince,
    there be two sorts of niggers:
    those who give the whip and those who taste it.

OKO:

    The forest of my boyhood is dense.
    Creepers cover the branches;
    ancient roots lace the ground.
    I do not care that you make
    a map of the biggest forest of the land
    upon my torn back.
    Let lianas crawl forlorn from branch
    to darkening branch
    till they choke for want of light.

DRIVER: *(Laughs)*

    I see your forest once. It is enough.

OKO:

    Imoinda has been gone
    these many moons past.
    I demand to know of her.

DRIVER:

    What number you wear on your shoulder?
    (Drumsbeat)

OKO:

    One o one.

DRIVER:
> Who put it there?

OKO:
> Not you, else
> you would have swallowed teeth first.

DRIVER:
> You threaten Driver? You not season well!
> Massa don't like slave threatening Driver.
> The ground in your hut too comfortable
> for you to rest your back?

OKO:
> I demand to know where Imoinda is.

DRIVER:
> That is big word. It is not for slave.

OKO:
> Where is Imoinda?

DRIVER:
> No slave call so.

OKO:
> You know full well.

DRIVER:
> No slave call so.

OKO:
> So, they've called her some other name.
> She is my Imoinda.

DRIVER:
> No slave call so.

OKO:
Clemene?

DRIVER:
She go with Massa Boss brother.
She present for his bride, maybe.
She make his bed? She in his bed?

OKO:
There is no other word for you but "dog!"

(They fight. Men gather and follow the action with muffled sound. Gunshot. Silence. Enter OVERSEER and two slaves)

OVERSEER:
Pincher! Bigger! Hold that slave fast!
Slave more full of airs I have not seen.
Bind him fast I say!

OKO:
I must know of Imoinda.

OVERSEER:
What gibberish is this?

OKO:
She is my wife.

OVERSEER:
Your wife? You have papers to prove this?
The marks on your shoulder, the initials
says you are slave number one o one,
the property of this plantation.

Even the fingers on your hands
you cannot claim.

All were purchased by another.
Your wife?
Driver what is this ruckus all about?

DRIVER:

He say he want his wife. *(Drums and sticks)*
He say he make me swallow my teeth.

OVERSEER:

Damn and blast those interferers!
Now, this slave has been so badly seasoned
he wreaks chaos where he walks.

DRIVER:

It is Massa Boss brother, Overseer.

OVERSEER:

I know! More money than common sense.
Fifty lashes! The only way he'll learn.
And he stays the night in the stocks.
The grounds of the Great House
are out of bounds on pain of death. Driver!

DRIVER:

Yes, Massa Overseer.

OVERSEER:

You two assist Driver.
Pincher, you can count.
Fifty lashes no more no less
and report to me when all is done.
There's a pair of breeches in it
for each of you tonight.
This slave called Caesar will be taught
to know well his masters and his betters.
(Exits. Whipcracks)

Act Three Scene 1

CHORUS:

One! (*Sound — Drums and sticks*)
Better to forget the past sooner.
Two!
If you don't, your body will be broken.
Three!
After all is one body for one man.
Four!
And what does overseer care?
Five!
Is not his money buying.
Six!
Is not his body burning.
Seven!
When the body bruk up.
Eight!
Things still not easy.
Nine!
If you live you can fight again.
Ten!
If you can walk, you can run.
Eleven!
But if you maim and foot gone.
Twelve !
Who go run for you?
(*Lights fade. Superimposed image of the whip on a body of slaves*)
Always the whip! Always the whip!
Marking our bodies lest we forget.
Always the whip! Always the whip!
Scourging our memories lest we remember.
Always the whip! Always the whip!
Teaching the lesson we dare not forget. (*An agonised howl*)

disciplining of racialized bodies

76

Scene 2

Imoinda's return to the plantation is made especially busy with preparations for MASSA's forthcoming wedding. The evening prior to the wedding party for MASSA BOSS BROTHER and OKO acts to secure Imoinda's attention. In the shadow of the Great House, as the band practises, a figure of four is made by a group of slaves including IMOINDA and ESTEIZME. Quadrille or other period dance MUSIC heavily backed by drums.

IMOINDA:
> I must go to him. Don't say otherwise.
> I vow to go to him.

ESTEIZME:
> When? Let me fix your anisa, your headtie.

IMOINDA
> I'd go this minute if I could, or tonight.

ESTEIZME:
> Smile. Look carefree while you plan.

IMOINDA:
> I cannot. I share his torture too much.

ESTEIZME:
> Of course. But when is best?

IMOINDA:
> Under cover of darkness.
> The Great House will probably be full.
> But will I be missed?

ESTEIZME:
> Is there a better time then?

IMOINDA:
No. Bring me herbs before darkness falls
that I might make a poultice
to ease his sorry wounds.
About the other matter,
there is little easing I can do.

ESTEIZME:
You drank the bush tea at the right time?

IMOINDA:
I drink bitter bush each day.

ESTEIZME:
I speak of medicine.

IMOINDA:
I drank. How I drank!

ESTEIZME:
Still you do not see your days?

IMOINDA:
No.

ESTEIZME:
How many moons has it been?

IMOINDA:
I am not sure; I wish I could say
but, Esteizme, I must tell him.

ESTEIZME:
And you sure this baby is not his?

IMOINDA:
How could it be his?

ESTEIZME:
>   Smile as you speak. You are sure?

IMOINDA:
>   I have not known Prince Oko
>   since we set foot upon this land.

ESTEIZME:
>   Tonight we women will dance for you.
>   We'll call upon Mama Aisa.
>   The gods of our ancestors know best.

DRIVER: *(Enters)*
>   What! You two prattling in your tongue?

ESTEIZME:
>   It is the same tongue you understand.

DRIVER:
>   No. Yours, woman, stay too sharp.
>   Silence! This not holiday; *(Esteizme glowers)*
>   work waiting fuh done.
>   And you, Clemene, grow round;
>   inside the Great House, you fatten. *(Esteizme growls)*
>   Go gather fruits for massa table
>   and quick sharp! Plenty fuh do!
>   *(They exit. Enters overseer)*

OVERSEER:
>   Work, song, dance and slave don't mix.
>   But tomorrow back to the old order.
>   *(MUSIC resumes)*
>   And send the girl, Clemene to me.

DRIVER:
>   Yes, Massa Overseer. *(Exits. IMOINDA enters)*

OVERSEER:
Go fetch some water for my tub.

IMOINDA:
But . . .

OVERSEER:
I brook neither ifs nor buts.
(Light fades. Dance MUSIC plays)

Scene 3: Indoors.
The last rays of light falls through an open window.

OVERSEER:
Come, come! A little more water.
(MUSIC — "New Land" Theme)
That's better. Bring that screen here.
Wouldn't do for me to catch a chill.
By the by, a new frock lies yonder.

IMOINDA:
Yes, massa?

OVERSEER:
Try it on.

IMOINDA:
Massa, what I trying on more?

OVERSEER:
An order. Open the trunk. Take it up.
(Collects frock and goes to door)
I never told you to leave the room.

IMOINDA:
But massa. Look my hands. Wet and . . .

OVERSEER:
(Indicates screen)
Yes? Quite a player of games, mistress "But"!
Change there, as you wish, but be quick about it.
Damn it, wench. Come, scrub my feet.
See what strong feet an overseer needs have.

(Imoinda emerges in a low cut frock. She bends at the tub. Overseer grins)

IMOINDA:
> Feet of hunter.

OVERSEER:
> Nothing so savage. Here's the soap.
> Mind you work a good lather about my toes.
> Splendid. You bed in this house from tonight.

IMOINDA:
> Massa, I have jobs in slave quarters.

OVERSEER:
> Soap! From this night, your job is to serve me.
> Plenty to do here, too. Bring the soap.

IMOINDA:
> Massa! *(Hands the soap. Overseer clasps her wrists)*

OVERSEER:
> So, this frock fits you well.
> Stand. Study the glass.
> A picture! Thank you massa!

IMOINDA:
> Thank you massa. Massa finished?

OVERSEER:
> I am not finished! Scrub your hunter's back.
> *(She scrubs viciously)*
> A man's appetite is all. *(Drums)*
> Now, the towel. Don't stand there looking dumb.
> Fetch it! Hold it up. And in the tub!

IMOINDA:
> Please, I'd sooner bathe in other waters.
> *(Grabs and strips her)*

OVERSEER:
>But you will wallow right here in my tub!
>Some nigger smell to make you feel at home.
>*(Drops old frock into tub. Secures her. Blows out the
>lamp. A stone crashes through the window)*

IMOINDA:
>Mercy!

OVERSEER:
>Mercy? Now why do you plead mercy?
>*(Pins IMOINDA against wall)*
>Tell me, just whose hand do you see in this,
>little vixen, little manicou?

IMOINDA:
>I do not know.

OVERSEER:
>Which one? Speak, or taste the whip this night.

IMOINDA:
>I cannot tell what I do not know.

OVERSEER:
>A likely story.

DRIVER's Voice:
>Massa Overseer! Massa Overseer!

IMOINDA:
>Do I clean up now, massa? *(Dresses hastily)*

OVERSEER:
>At least one of those lusting devils
>*(MUSIC — "Always the Whip")*
>will live long enough to know regret.

Scene 4: The plantation

Another corner of the Great House. MUSIC — practice in preparation for wedding.

IMOINDA:
>Oko, say it was not you.
>There is death upon the head of any
>who attempts the Overseer's life.

OKO:
>Once before I should have killed for you.
>Now to watch you with others is death.

IMOINDA:
>Not so. Don't let us quarrel.

OKO:
>Imoinda, I hunger
>for the taste of you.
>Even when I let work blot you out
>it is but a poor trick;
>a lie my body knows.
>I fancy being dead may be better.

IMOINDA:
>Don't say that. Without you I cannot live.

OKO:
>Has he touched you before?

IMOINDA:
>No.

OKO:
>When you were away, did anyone?

IMOINDA:

Hush! Make less noise! Hush!
Why summon those dogs to your funeral?

OKO:

Did anyone? But first, let me taste you.
Why do you keep such distance between us?

IMOINDA:

Distance? Sometimes it's safer.
It doesn't lessen the longing that I feel.

OKO:

Though these hands are less soft than they were
and your skin's lost its sheen of ripe berry
and the fire in your eyes burn less bright,
I remember well. Now, let me taste you. *(They kiss)*
What is this mound between us?
(MUSIC - "Moon Witness, Enchanted Night" Theme)
Between us stands a mound of belly
that was not there before. Alas!
Imoinda, I remember you
every part, every texture, every curve.

IMOINDA:

Yes! I am a slave woman; game to all.
Don't close your eyes. It is what you see.

OKO:

I will kill the bastard with these bare hands,
then die like a man.

IMOINDA:

Make less noise! *(MUSIC — "Enchanted Night")*

OKO:

> The Overseer? Did you want him?

VOICES:

> Hunt him down!
> There is something in it
> for he who first finds him.

IMOINDA:

> Oko, fly! Run!

VOICE:

> Bring the slave Caesar! To me!

OKO:

> No I'll die first; but so will he.

IMOINDA:

> Oko, fly! Run!

OKO:

> I think I know this trick. It stinks.
> I'm out of the way;
> You can take lovers all you please.

IMOINDA:

> Oko, you should know me better.

OKO:

> Call me Caesar.
> You belong to Caesar and who else?
> What a fine gown you wear while I'm in rags.

IMOINDA:

> Oko.

OKO:

    Caesar!

IMOINDA:

    Caesar, run, hide. There is life in us yet.
    Take the path by the tamarind tree.
    I'll hold them here. Run, I implore you.

OKO:

    Get me a knife. I am still a warrior.
    (OKO exits. MUSIC — "Triumph of Manhood")

OVERSEER:

    Where is the slave, Caesar?

IMOINDA:

    I do not know; I cannot say.

OVERSEER:

    We find him tonight,
    by conch blow at dawn, he hangs
    by one leg; an example to you all. *(Echoes of "New Land" with conch)*

Scene 5

Later that evening, Imoinda finds Oko caged. He demands a knife. MUSIC — "New Land".

WOMAN:
This land drinks blood. How it thirsts after it!
Was ever nation born without blood?
Was ever new nation drank blood as this?

IMOINDA:
I bring food. Can you not sit up?

OKO:
I do not need food. Rather, bring me leaves.

IMOINDA:
Leaves?

OKO:
To staunch the flow of blood.
My leg! *(MUSIC — "Triumph" theme)*
My leg is cut off. Quick, fetch the leaves.
And if I mean anything to you,
I must have the knife I asked for.
I am a Kromanti warrior yet.
A knife to sharpen these tough old claws.

(She removes a knife from underneath her anisa/ headtie and hands it to him)

IMOINDA:
If only I could hold you.

OKO:
Go quick; bring the leaves. *(She exits)*

WOMAN: *(Circles the cage)*
    This land drinks blood. How it thirsts after it!
    The blood of its native people cry out.
    But, was ever nation born without blood?

OKO:
    Come back warrior, I command you!
    Come back! I do not fear blood.
    So, all is lost; another warrior dies.
    (Stabs himself. Ritual dance. Drums and sticks)

WOMAN:
    This land drinks blood. How it thirsts after it!
    The blood of its native people cry out.

CHORUS:
    Oroonoko! Oroonoko!
    Triumph of Manhood. When such a son flies,
    must not all the nations dance as one?

IMOINDA: *(Re-enters. Whispers)*
    Oko! Oko! Why does he not answer?

WOMAN:
    My child, he travels to the ancestors.
    A warrior to the last. He goes well.

IMOINDA:
    No! Where is my man? *(MUSIC — "Enchanted Night")*
    My poor skin still cries for his fingertips.

(ESTEIZME enters dancing)

WOMAN:
    Don't ask us. Dance. Trust your eyes.
    Only shipmates you see before you
    all landed here from the nightmare canoe.

ESTEIZME:
>
> Heed the spirits. Trust your eyes.
> They speak through our bodies. You'll hear no lies.

IMOINDA:
>
> I'll tear this cage wide open
> so that our blood mingles and beside him
> I might know the taste of happy death.

ESTEIZME:
>
> Ease yourself a little. Dance.

IMOINDA:
>
> How I've ached for this man
> an ache so deep, so wide.
> Like a gorge cutting into my soul.
> No point, no point in living.

WOMAN:
>
> Can't get far from the nightmare canoe.
> *(MUSIC — "Nightmare Canoe")*
> It's made of my death wish,
> your death wish, their death wish.

CHORUS:
>
> After the nightmare canoe
> the silence of tongues cut out.
> There's still worse to come.
> And all our own questions ride the wind
> in silence!

IMOINDA:
>
> Leave me alone! Let me get the knife.

ESTEIZME:
>
> You have the pikin to think of.

IMOINDA:
> Death is better. Let me get the knife.
> *(She hurls herself at the cage door and falls panting, hand searching within)*

IMOINDA:
> I have seen beautiful humming birds
> *(Music - "Moon Witness")*
> sipping the life sustaining nectar.
> Just so once, I took all I needed.
> Now no more. The birds are free. Not me. *(Panting)*
>
> Dun coloured cows with baleful eyes
> stand still in the storm.
> They are bred as it suits their owners.
> Not me; I would rather die. *(Her panting quickens)*
>
> What is this pain that gnaws at my insides?
> Gracious death, I embrace you!
> Esteizme, take my hand.
> I feel a fierce burning deep inside me.

ESTEIZME
> Take my hand. Tighter. It is the pikin.

IMOINDA:
> Pikin? Baby? No. I will have none.
> Since I cannot have my man,
> I will not have another's pikin.

ESTEIZME:
> You have no choice.

IMOINDA:
> What life is this without choice? Birth here?
> To a pikin I would not have
> except I had been forced. What life is this?

I will not have a pikin in whose face
I'll see my own humiliation
every day. It is the massa's.
Let him scrape it from this blood fed soil. *(Panting)*

WOMAN:
(MUSIC — "Her Back A Bridge")
In order to cross the river
We first must build the bridge.

CHORUS:
And bridges come in different size,
shape and look but are bridges for all that.

WOMAN:
Your back, my child is a bridge.
Push! Let it come. Let it breathe.

IMOINDA:
No! Unless I know it is a son
to wreak rough vengeance upon a father.
Besides, I'll have none but a warrior.

WOMAN:
Your back, my child is a bridge.

CHORUS:
And bridges come in different size,
shape and look but are bridges for all that.

WOMAN:
Your back, my child is a bridge.
Push! Let it come. Let it breathe.

IMOINDA:
> No! No! Not in this cursed place!
> No! I say again. Not in this cursed place!
> Not yet! Not ever! Noooooooooooo!

WOMAN:
> *(MUSIC — "Sleeping Volcanoes")*
> Your back, my child is a bridge.
> Push! Let it come. Let it breathe. *(Women circle)*

WOMEN:
> Push! Let it come. Let it breathe.
> We sleeping volcanoes; we women.

CHORUS:
> We slumbering volcanoes,
> seemingly so unmoved and unmoving.

WOMEN:
> See how serene we seem at times to be;
> beautiful even, some moments.
> Push! Let it come. Let it breathe!

IMOINDA:
> No! Cover me in coconut branches
> when I die.

WOMEN:
> We sleeping volcanoes; we women.

CHORUS:
> Sleeping volcanoes; our women, our men
> and when we erupt, rumble
> spit stones of words; pour fires of rage
> then you know we are not stone.

WOMEN:
>Then you may know we sleeping volcanoes
>are tender, thoughtful, suffering
>but not endlessly.

IMOINDA:
>Bury me beneath. Ahhh!
>*(Screams. A baby's cry is heard)*

ESTEIZME:
>No! Not yet death! Listen! A baby's cry!

WOMAN:
>New life! Where there is new life there is hope.

ESTEIZME:
>A girl! And hope for new life again.

IMOINDA:
>A girl? Will all you she-gods not hear me?
>A girl born subject to such misery!

WOMAN:
>Yet it is life given; for one taken.
>This land may still claim the final victory.

IMOINDA:
>Though this be only life of sorts,
>in this new place, I have chosen life.
>*(They pass the baby round)*
>*(MUSIC — "Tasted Sorrow" theme)*

CHORUS:
>River Volta:
>Listen!
>River Nile:
>Listen!

River Gambia:
Listen!
River Niger:
Listen!
River Congo:
Listen!
The waters of five rivers:
Listen!
Witness a first rite completed.

CHORUS:
We chose life, a baby to wear red
in necklace or amulet;
a baby charged not to forget.
Here's a baby charged not to forget.

IMOINDA:
Though this be only life of sorts
They shall not have the final victory.
I have chosen life.

(Conch blows. MUSIC — "We Have Chosen Life". Lights fade)

IMOINDA: OR SHE WHO WILL LOSE HER NAME

Imoinda Or She Who Will Lose Her Name is a rewriting of Aphra Behn's seventeenth century text, *Oroonoko or the Royal Slave*. It was written as a libretto central to which is Imoinda, the hitherto silenced black woman figure in Behn's novel. *Imoinda* may thus be seen as an (alter)native though complimentary narrative. Giovanna Covi who first translated Anim-Addo's libretto with Chiara Pedrotti writes:

> Imoinda is related to Oroonoko in obvious and also surprising ways: written in response to Behn's novel, Anim-Addo's libretto is not only influenced by the original text, does not simply write the story back from the point of view of 'the other' female character; most importantly, it subversively revises the very reality that inspired Behn's fiction. (2002: 83)

Chronology
1996 Talawa Theatre – Women Writers' Bursary Award during which *Imoinda* was developed.
1998 Rehearsed reading, Oval House Theatre, London, 19 June. Director, Warren Wills.
1999 Performance (Extract), Horniman Museum (The Conservatory), 1 August. Director, Juwon Ogungbe.
2003 First published – bi-lingual edition – *Imoinda: Or She Who Will Lose Her Name – A Play for Twelve Voices in Three Acts / Imoinda, Colei Che Perder Il Nome – Opera dodici voci in tre atti*, translated by Giovanna Covi & Chiara Pedrotti, in Covi, Giovanna, ed., *Voci femminili caraibiche e interculturalita*, (Trento : Editrice Universita degli Studi di Trento, 2003, 1-155. ISBN 88-8843-042-9. *I Labirinti*, Appendix, 1-155).
2007 School of the Arts (SOTA), Rochester, New York, 3-5 May. Composer, Glenn McClure.

Selected Writings about *Imoinda: Or She Who Will Lose Her Name*
Covi, Giovanna. "*Oroonoko*'s Genderization and Creolization: Joan Anim-Addo's **Imoinda**". *In Revisiting and Reinterpreting Aphra Behn*: Proceedings of the Aphra Behn Europe Seminar ESSE Conference, Entrevaux, France: Bilingua GA Editions, 2002, pp. 83-92.
Guarracino, Serena. "Imoinda's Performing Bodies: An Interview with Joan Anim-Addo. " In *I Am Black/White/ Yellow: An Introduction to the Black Body in Europe*, London: Mango Publishing, 2007, pp. 212-23.

About the Author
Joan Anim-Addo was born in Grenada. She is Director of the Centre for Caribbean Studies and a Senior Lecturer at Goldsmiths, University of London. Her writing includes poetry, history, literary criticism and drama. She is the author of six books and co-author of a further two titles. She has edited several collections of critical essays on Caribbean women's writing. Her most recent publications are *Janie, Cricketing Lady* (2006) and *Touching the Body: History, Language and Caribbean Women's Writing* (2007).